JUDGES POSTCARDS
A brief history

There is every chance that the postcard you send home from your holiday started life in Sussex. Since 1904 Hastings has been the home of Judges, one of Britain's leading publishers of quality picture postcards.

When Fred Judge arrived in Hastings in 1902 he could have had little idea of the worldwide impact he was to make on the business of postcard publishing. But Fred was a master with a camera and a natural entrepreneur. Fred Judge was born in Yorkshire in 1872. Photography was always his real interest, and it was while visiting Sussex in 1902 that he made the decision to give up engineering for a career as a photographer.

Fred and his brother Thomas purchased an existing business in Hastings and set up as photographers and photographic dealers under the name of Judge's Photo Stores. Although the idea of sending an illustrated card through the post was not new (the first having appeared towards the end of the nineteenth century) Fred made his mark by setting himself extremely high artistic standards. At first he concentrated on local scenes and activities. Having taken his pictures he would go straight back to the darkroom to make them into postcards – often for sale within a few hours; and the quality of his work was such that passers by would gather outside the shop window for a sight of his latest work.

Technically stunning, and using all the latest photographic technology, Fred's pictures won over 100 medals, and one-man exhibitions of his work were held in London, Washington, New York and Tokyo.

Back in Hastings the business was expanding, necessitating moves to bigger and better premises, culminating in the move in 1927 to the purpose-built factory that the company occupies to this day. Although the building has been developed and extended, the Italianate façade remains a famous landmark on the A259 coast road.

Fred Judge died in February 1950 at the age of 78, having built up an internationally respected company. The business was sold to another Judges photographer, who introduced lithographic colour printing. Then in 1984 Judges became a real family concern once again when Bernard and Jan Wolford took over. It became even more of a family business when their son Graeme, now managing director, joined, followed by Trevor, now sales director. The present management can truly be said to be building on the foundations laid by Fred Judge over ninety years ago.

Judges Postcards Ltd, 176 Bexhill Road, St Leonards on Sea,
East Sussex, TN38 8BN
Tel: 01424 420919; Fax: 01424 438538

YORKSHIRE

IN OLD PHOTOGRAPHS

DAVE RANDLE

FROM THE JUDGES POSTCARD ARCHIVE COLLECTION

SUTTON PUBLISHING

Sutton Publishing Limited
Phoenix Mill · Thrupp · Stroud
Gloucestershire · GL5 2BU

First published 2003
This edition published in 2005

British Library Cataloguing in Publication Data
A catalogue record for this book is available from
the British Library.

ISBN 0-7509-4160-X

Typeset in 11/13.5 Sabon.
Typesetting and origination by
Sutton Publishing Limited.
Printed and bound in England by
J.H. Haynes & Co. Ltd, Sparkford.

Introduction

Not only England's largest, but also one of its most diverse counties, Yorkshire is a place of grandeur, both scenic and historic. The rugged crags, the sheltered valleys, the raging falls and the meandering streams that provide spiritual satisfaction for today's visitor made it the most perfectly adapted landscape for early settlers.

Kings, barons and bishops flocked to its ready-fortified higher ground, adding their own wooden palisades and stone bastions to pike and promontory. Freemen, serfs and villeins huddled in the dales and coastal coves, making honest livings from its soil, its minerals, its fisheries and its grazing; others, less honest, from contraband and brigandry.

The forces of tumbling watercourses were harnessed by mill and leat for food and clothing and, ultimately, to turn the wheels of the industrial revolution. Holy men and women established simple communities by its peaceful streams and raised monumental minsters to their God.

For centuries disruptive forces came to make life difficult or impossible for all strata of life in the 'Ridings' – Romans, Saxons, Vikings, Lancastrians, Tudors and Stuarts – but in few places in the realm was the harmony of man and landscape as steadfastly protected and preserved as here.

Betimes stubborn, invariably indomitable and often possessed of an inscrutable sense of humour, the archetypical Yorkshire character both formed and was itself moulded by the dynamics of the landscape and the struggle to hold a position against various outside forces. In a county sharing its latitude with Copenhagen and Minsk, these forces could often be as elemental or meteorological as they were political.

Of course, its proximity to Scandinavia has played an especially significant part in defining the county and its people. When the Vikings came to Britain they came this way. So the great city of York, like London or Canterbury, owes its share to the Britons, the Romans, the Normans, et al, but, unlike them, was not just an object of attack but a centre of culture for the Vikings. With the discoveries made at York in the 1960s and the redefinition of the 'visitor experience' pioneered there, the name of Jorvik is again known far and wide.

Nowhere has a greater wealth of abbeys and ecclesiastical buildings of all kinds. Many now lie in ruins as a result of the Dissolution of the Monasteries enacted by Henry VIII. But often that is not the whole story. The materials for these medieval masterpieces were brought by land, sea, river and, in some cases, specially constructed canals, from places as far away as Caen in Normandy. The architectural plans, the scaffolding, the tools and the expertise to wield them were generated 'in-house' by the monks themselves. They were working at the forefront of contemporary technology. The sheer scale of the project would entail years of labour, but the failures and attendant redesigns inherent in innovation turned years to decades. Workers died in accidents, others simply of old age, long before their work came to fruition.

When the monasteries were outlawed by Henry in the 1530s many had stood for hundreds of years. Some had grown richer, others barely made ends meet. Most now suffered summary destruction, though a few in Yorkshire sidestepped the threat by becoming parish churches, and others, such as Selby Abbey, miraculously escaped the fate that befell others up and down the land.

What was left by Henry's agents was usually further dismantled by those in need of a bit of furniture or decent stone in their own houses. On the other hand, Yorkshire has an equally long tradition of landowners and visionaries who have contributed money and effort toward their preservation.

Yorkshire and its neighbour across the Pennines were the cradle of the industrial revolution. From the middle ages onward there seems to have been a mill of some sort every few hundred yards on some of the county's rivers. Fulling mills, flour mills, paper mills were everywhere – and the inventiveness of the millers in exploiting the power of the waterwheels led to the development of wooden toothed gears and leather band drives that formed the basis of factory engineering.

Sheffield and Bradford led the world in this field. Sheffield plate, stainless steel, cranes, boilers, engines – their fame spread throughout the industrialising world. And Yorkshire had the steel on tap, along with lead and coal and the other ingredients of the new economy.

Wool making and dyeing and fishing and farming went on, but the world had changed and Yorkshire with it – if not before it. The great docks on the Humber at Hull delivered the new goods to that waiting world. Wool ceased to be exported, but was now imported from Australia and New Zealand, to be spun and worsted and dyed here.

But another thread has run through Yorkshire's history, and it is as vital an element of Yorkshireness as any other. It is an innate sense of order; of knowing what is right – the core certainty that has enabled its people to preserve its harmonious nature through the upheavals of the past. It could be described as the Betty's Tea Rooms factor – a provincial gentility with the force to flatten a bloodthirsty rabble.

See how Richmond, Harrogate and York impose concord on the wild and chaotic landscape. Gates, bars and dwellings are placed with pinpoint precision for the glory and aesthetic pleasure of mankind. The disorder, the vastness, the sense of uncontrollability, all has been scaled down and made unassailably pleasant and proper.

This first selection from the Judges Postcards archive covers the broad sweep of the county, from sparsely populated valleys to the boiling cauldron of Sheffield at its industrial height. There are plenty of opportunities for nostalgia and for glorying in or mourning bygone days, but there is also continuity; the reassurance that much that was good is still with us.

Nowhere has more effort gone into preserving and comprehending the past. These photographs, many of which have not been seen in years, make a substantial contribution to recent history and our store of knowledge.

YORKSHIRE

IN OLD PHOTOGRAPHS

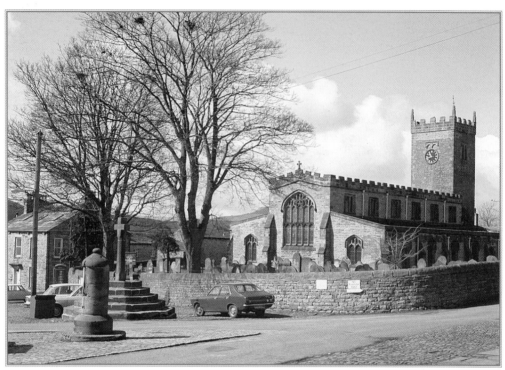

This is Askrigg's St Oswald's church in the 1970s. The present building goes back to the 1400s, though the village itself predates the Norman Conquest, and once had its own bullring. Askrigg was the setting for the BBC series based on James Herriot's vet books.

The River Bain, on which Bainbridge stands, is the shortest river in Britain. By 700-year-old tradition, in the winter months a horn is sounded at nine o'clock every evening on the village green to provide orientation for anyone still abroad on the fells.

Bedale in the late 1960s. Its wide street plan going back to medieval times was designed for markets and fairs but now provides ideal parking for its many visitors.

Mary Queen of Scots was held at Bolton Castle in 1568. It has been a ruin since the seventeenth century, though some renovation has gone on in recent years, and it now contains a Dales Museum.

One of the greatest tourist attractions in the Dales, Aysgarth Falls descends in a series of three steps, known as 'forces'. This is Upper Force.

At one time the area of Wensleydale around Bolton Castle was heavily mined for coal and lead. Nowadays it has returned to more pastoral uses.

The so-called Bridestones at Staindale are standing rocks once regarded as fertility symbols. Offerings and prayers to the 'brides' encouraged fruitfulness and good harvests, so it was believed.

Burnsall, in Wharfedale, is the home of England's oldest fell race. There are some old Norse gravestones and the village stocks are preserved in the churchyard.

Opposite: A popular centre for touring and horseriding, Buckden, in Upper Wharfedale, gets its name from the fact that it was occupied by the foresters in charge of Langrothsdale Chace. The name 'forest' originally meant 'hunting reserve' and Buckden was the site of the 'buck-den' – 'deer-enclosure' in Norman and Saxon times.

Star of countless film and television productions – in particular, Granada's *Brideshead Revisited* – Castle Howard was built by playwright-cum-architect Sir John Vanbrugh in the early years of the eighteenth century. Equally famous for his restoration comedies, such as *The Provok'd Wife*, Vanbrugh was also Sir Christopher Wren's principal colleague. Blenheim Palace in Oxfordshire is his other great work.

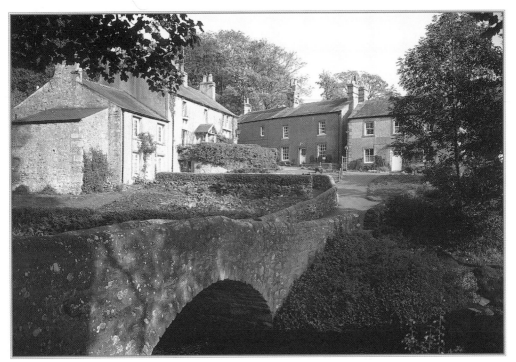

Clapham in Lonsdale stands at the foot of Ingleborough mountain, from which it gets
its name – 'clopp', meaning a big hill, and 'ham', meaning a home or farmstead.
The majority of visitors are drawn by Ingleborough Cave, which connects with Gaping
Gill pothole.

A view of Constable Burton in the 1970s. The village owes its existence to nearby
Burton Hall, ancestral home of the Constable family, set in a park to the north laid out
by Lancelot 'Capability' Brown.

Springtime in Crayke, near Easingwold. The Bishops of Durham had a fortress here and its fifteenth-century Great Chamber still survives in the bailey of the old Norman castle. York Minster is visible from the highest point.

Sheep graze in Danby village in the 1970s. Henry VIII's sixth wife Catherine Parr once owned the castle here.

Opposite: This picture of the famous Duck Bridge in Eskdale and its nearby stepping stones in the 1970s could have been taken at almost any time in the last thousand years, although the fact that it is a photograph narrows it down a bit. Its name has nothing to do with ducks, but refers to George Duck, who had it repaired in the eighteenth century.

A paradise for walkers and ramblers today, the Dalby and Keldy forests were once hunting grounds for Norman barons. Now they are managed for the protection of the wildlife.

Thirteen miles from York, Easingwold is an old market town of cobbles and red brick. Its name probably means the wood of Esa's people, though it could derive from a Saxon word for flooding.

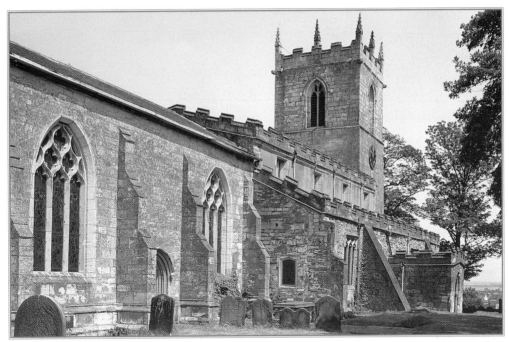

Epworth is famous as the home of Methodists John and Charles Wesley. The church was built in 1889 as a memorial to them and features a stained glass window of the two looking toward the rectory in which they were born.

The Old Rectory at Epworth is now a Wesleyan museum. The present building dates from 1709, the original rectory having been destroyed by arsonists prior to that date.

The huge church at Egton Bridge is dedicated to the Catholic Saint Edda. Built in 1866, it commemorates Father Nicholas Postgate, who was martyred at York for baptising a child at his house in the village.

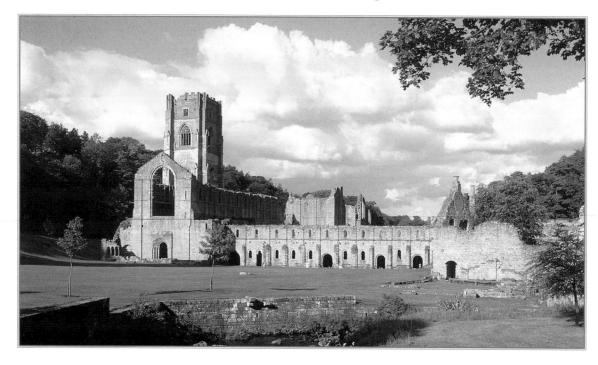

These falls at Gayle are naturally known as Gayle Force. The village is an important producer of the famous Wensleydale cheese.

Opposite: One of the most important monasteries in Britain at the time of the dissolution (1540), Fountains Abbey's ruinous state is as much the work of local landowners as jealous monarchs. Built over decades in the 'Vale of the Fountains' by the monks, its remains have been used as a ready supply of building materials for centuries. In 1611 Sir Stephen Proctor dismantled the infirmary and used it to build Fountains Hall, which also contains furniture from the abbey.

The story goes that a beggar named Tom Ferris fell in love with a girl from the other side of the River Esk. For much of the year the river was impossible to cross so they were separated. Having later bettered his position in a big way by becoming mayor of Hull, he returned to Glaisdale, married the girl and built Beggar's Bridge.

Goathland in the 1970s. Its squat church and mainly grey stone houses straggled across wide areas of open grass suggest this was always a peaceful, untroubled place. It is a favourite location for Yorkshire Television's period police series *Heartbeat*.

Crossing point of the River Wharfe since medieval times, Grassington is known as the 'capital of Upper Wharfedale'. Its stone bridge was originally built in 1603, though it has been widened and flattened in later years.

Gunnerside is a peaceful village these days beloved of walkers and trippers, but for many years its villagers partook in the poisoned prosperity brought to it by local lead mines.

Harewood House dates from 1767. Both it and much of its furniture are the work of Adam, and the grounds are by Capability Brown. It boasts a lake and a collection of exotic birds in addition to the paintings and other treasures to be viewed inside the house.

The mainly Victorian spa town of Harrogate thrives today as an ideal location for conferences. Its annual festival in August also draws music lovers from all points of the compass. The Valley Gardens, seen here in the 1960s, form part of over 200 acres of greenery in and around the town.

The Royal Baths at Harrogate before the First World War. The curative waters and the clean, bracing air were the main ingredients in the town's fame and the reasons for its expansion in Victorian times.

Betty's Tea Rooms in Harrogate (along with its counterpart in York) is known far and wide. Nobody's really sure who Betty was. The business was actually established by Charles Taylor, the Yorkshire Tea man, and a Swiss-born Belgian chocolatier called Frederick Belmont.

Opposite: Prospect Place, Harrogate, in the 1970s, with the war memorial and the post office at the far end.

Not much changes in the steadfast stone-built town of Hawes, but these pictures are pure 1960s. Standing on the Pennine Way, it is the second highest market town in England.

The Pennine Way at Hawes in the 1980s.

The watermill at Hawes with the Wensleydale dairy beyond the bridge in around 1920.

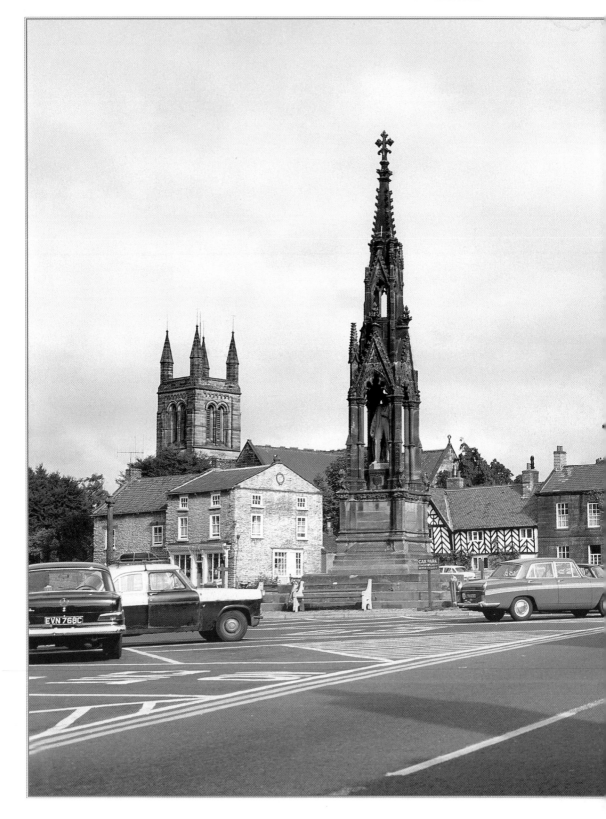

The market place in Helmsley at the end of the 1960s, looking toward the Crown Inn and the Pheasant Hotel.

Helmsley church retains its Norman porch, but the main body of the building dates from the nineteenth century and the stained glass is modern.

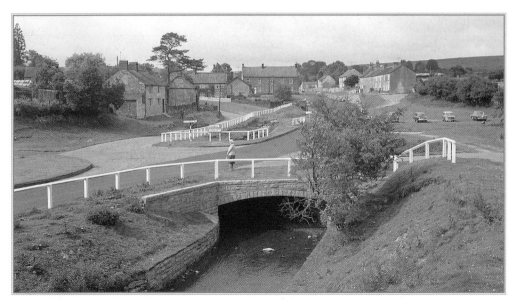

Considered one of the most picturesque villages in Yorkshire, Hutton-le-Hole has become a showplace of Dales life. Apart from those reconstructed in the Ryedale Folk Museum, its oldest building is Quaker Cottage, built in 1693 and belonging to John Richardson, a friend of William Penn, founder of Pennsylvania.

'On Ilkley Moor baht 'at' is Yorkshire's contribution to the traditional British pub singalong. That somebody should write a song about someone who went on to the moor without a hat would seem to suggest that not much out of the ordinary happened here in times past. Some time in the 1970s these people went hatless into Ilkley town centre, although one of them did have an umbrella.

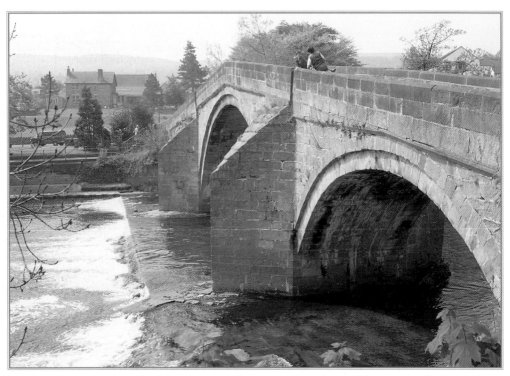

The elegant triple-arched bridge over the River Wharfe at Ilkley was built in 1673.

One of Upper Wharfedale's most impressive landmarks, Kilnsey Crag is the venue for an
annual 'crag race'. Here it looms over the Tennant Arms in the 1980s.

The White Horse on the hillside above Kilburn was carved out by pupils from the local school in 1857, under the supervision of their schoolmaster, John Hodgson.

The 'Mouseman's Cottage' was the home of Robert 'Mousey' Thompson, so called from the trademark carved mouse he added to his work in seven hundred of England's churches – including the one in Kilburn – as well as York Minster and Westminster Abbey. The cottage contains his original domestic furniture. Wood carving is still carried on in Kilburn.

Overlooking the River Aire, Kirkstall Abbey still retains much of its Norman grandeur. Built for the Cistercians by Abbot Alexander, it was completed at the end of the twelfth century.

Listed in the Domesday Book, Kirkbymoorside's origins go back a lot further than the Normans. Remains of prehistoric man and animals have been found in the area and there are cairns on nearby hills. The Duke of Buckingham, George Villiers, died here and is immortalised in the church records as 'Gorge Viluas, Lord Dooke of bockingham'. He made and spent a fortune in his life and was cared for in his penury at the end by a villager. Here are the Swan, the White Horse and the Westminster Bank in the 1960s.

Walter l'Espec founded Kirkham Priory on the banks of the Derwent in the twelfth century. The Augustinians flourished here for three centuries and its thirteenth-century gatehouse contains some heraldic shields.

The market place in Knaresborough in the 1970s. Particularly well known for linen making, the town is largely Georgian in style, though it was here in Saxon times and is a royal borough. The chemist's shop has been in continuous use since 1720, so can claim to be the oldest in England.

The River Nidd at Knaresborough. Near the town is the curious Dropping Well, which calcifies objects placed in its path. A collection of petrified parasols, cuddly toys, gloves and hats hangs in its entrance.

Malham Cove is one of the most spectacular limestone formations in England. The village nestles in the valley, where Malham Beck is crossed by three clapper bridges.

Opposite: Lastingham and a local collie frozen in time. The crypt of St Mary's church was originally part of a Benedictine abbey built by two monks who came here from Lindisfarne in the seventh century. Cedd and Chad were brothers and were both later canonised. The abbey was destroyed by the Danes in the middle of the ninth century.

On Langton Wold without a (hard) hat in the 1970s. Malton's livestock market is one of the biggest in England. For the last two centuries it has also been known for its thoroughbred horses.

Opposite: As well as St Michael's parish church, the market place at Malton also features a Roman museum containing finds from the fortress that once stood on this site. Apart from the cars, little has changed between the earlier picture from the 1960s and the later, taken in the late 1980s.

Middleham formerly had two markets – a general one on the site still used today and the other, a pig market, marked with a second cross at West End. Like Malton, it is a centre for racehorse training.

The fortified bridge over the River Ure at Middleham.

Middleham Castle has one of the largest keeps in England. Built on the site of an earlier motte and bailey, it belonged to Richard III from 1471. Henry VII took it over following the Battle of Bosworth Field and it continued to be a royal castle until the beginning of the seventeenth century. This photograph was taken in the second decade of the twentieth century.

Newton-on-Rawcliffe is still mainly a farming village, though its remoteness, and the fact that it has often been omitted from maps, has exerted a paradoxical attraction to tourists. Rawcliffe is from the Saxon for red.

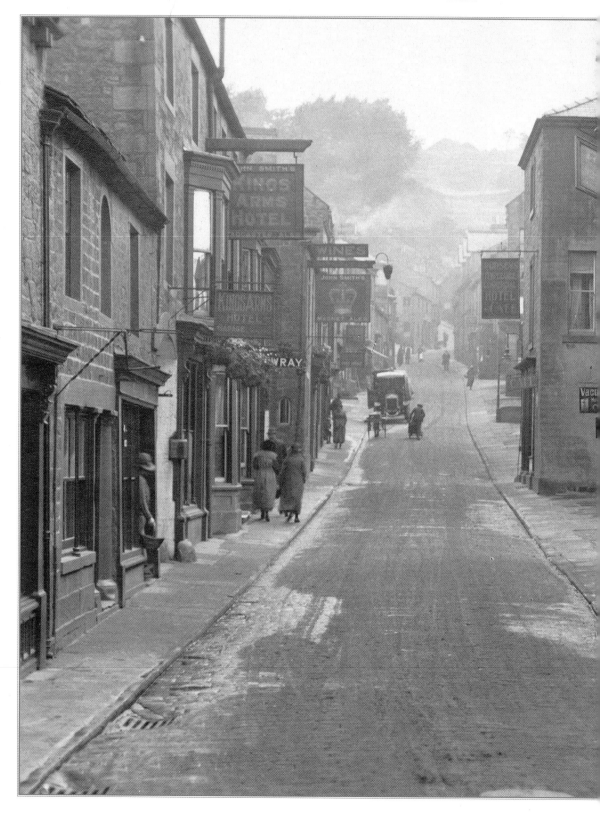

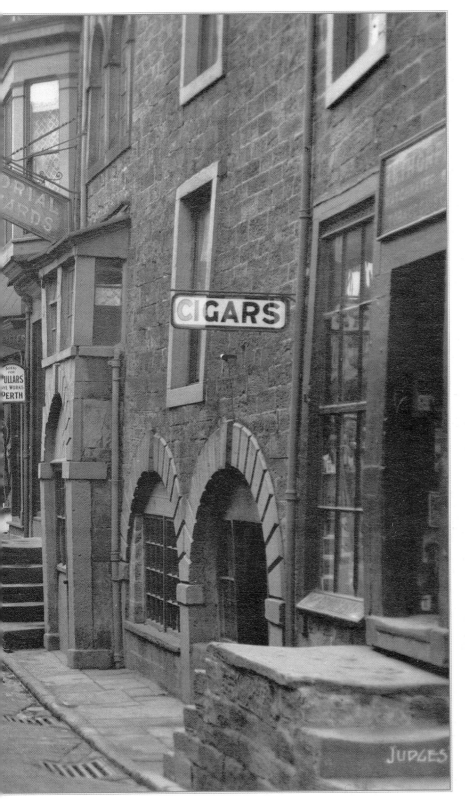

Pateley Bridge High Street in the 1920s, looking uphill to the Kings Arms and beyond. The photographer has wisely included the shop in which the postcard will be sold.

The same street in Pateley Bridge half a century later. There's no call any more for the 'mounting block' steps. Double yellow lines are the order of the day, though the traffic volume doesn't seem that much higher.

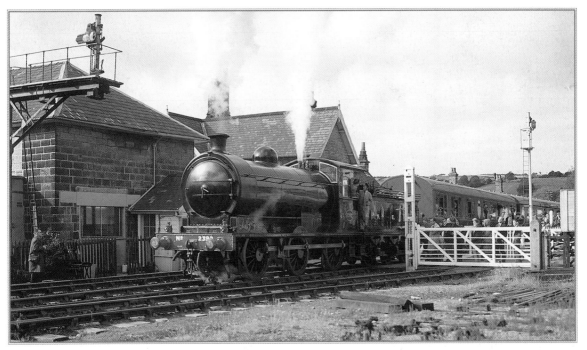

It would be hard to find a better location for a preserved steam railway than the North York Moors. These pictures show NER Class P3 0–6–0 number 2392 and LMS Class 5 4–6–0 number 45428. The line's Goathland station played an important supporting role in the film *Harry Potter and the Philosopher's Stone*, when it doubled as Hogsmead. The NYM Railway shop was the prefects' room and the ladies' toilets became the wizards' room.

The tortured rocks of Ribblesdale at Pen-Y-Ghent. Its summit is 2,273 feet above sea level.

Opposite: Pickering was first established by the Celts as far back as 270BC. Legend has it that the local king lost a ring in the river and it was found in the belly of a pike – hence pike-ring – an event depicted on the town's coat of arms. There are only a few years between the first picture here, taken in the 1960s, and the second from the 1970s, but it was enough time not only to paint the double yellow lines, but also for people to start parking on them.

These two shots of the Forest & Vale reveal some changes too, apart from the tall concrete lamp-post and the sudden sprouting of foliage on the terrace. The first is from the early 1960s; the second was taken in February 1999.

Pickering Castle, to the north of the town, was a hunting lodge in medieval times. It is now a picturesque ruin.

The castle, built in 1071 for Alun the Red, was designed to protect its Norman proprietor from both the Danes and the English. After all that, neither of them turned up. Don't you just hate that?

This extraordinary picture of Holy Trinity church, Richmond, before the First World
War shows shops and substantial buildings directly connected to the church tower.

Above: These buildings
were pulled down quite
soon afterward, as this
photograph shows.
The obelisk dates from
the eighteenth century.

Richmond's hill took some climbing in the days before motorised transport and a horse and cart could take some stopping on the way down. This is the way down to the old bridge in around 1920.

The lanes and alleys of The Bar still retain their charm. In the days before the First World War they were more organic and much less refined.

Here's Frenchgate in more recent times – 1980s – looking toward the castle. The buildings have been there forever, but they're neater now.

No longer used as a church from 1971, in 1973 Holy Trinity became home to the museum of the Green Howards Regiment.

Rievaulx Abbey was built in 1131 on land granted to the French Cistercian monks by Walter l'Espec, Lord of Helmsley – he was also responsible for Kirkham Priory. Its construction was a monumental task for the monks, who even built a canal nearby to bypass the non-navigable stretch of the River Rye, by which it stands and whence it gets its name.

A recent picture of Ripon Cathedral looking a little like Gulliver in the land of the
Lilliputians. There is a Saxon crypt beneath it dating back to 672, so this modern
housing will always seem insubstantial by comparison.

There was some kind of settlement in Ripon going back to Roman times, but the present city owes its origins to Eata, the Abbot of Melrose, who built the so-called Scots Monastery here in the latter half of the seventh century. A forest horn is sounded in the market square at nine each evening as part of a tradition going back a thousand years.

Eata was succeeded as Abbot by Wilfred, who set about modernising and fortifying the monastery with stone, and it is from his buildings that the cathedral evolved. Ripon was in a pretty bad state when the Normans' Domesday surveyors came round. They just wrote 'waste' over the area. But a new church was built and developed over the ensuing years and completed by Roger de Pont l'Eveque in 1181. Major restoration work was undertaken in the late nineteenth century and again in the 1950s.

The neo-classical frontage of Ripon's Town Hall in Kirkgate speaks of affluence owed by the city to the heyday of the wool trade. Another Ripon speciality not expected to make a comeback is spur-making.

Ripon Cathedral from Kirkgate.

Above: The precipitate approach to Robin Hood's Bay, often described as the Clovelly of the north, in the 1960s, before the Midland Bank had been shanghaied.

Ravenscar and Robin Hood's Bay from Old Peak or South Cheek – whichever you prefer. The next outcrop along, which provides the bay's northern arm, is known as The Ness or North Cheek. 'Ness', of course, means 'nose', to further complicate matters. There was a lighthouse here in Roman times.

Two views of the Quayside at Robin Hood's Bay. These were taken ten years before the new 40-foot-high sea wall was built, when it was not unusual for individual cottages or whole streets to slip away into the sea. Known locally as 'Bay Town', it has no known connections with Robin of Sherwood.

Sandsend, as the name might suggest, is where the beach runs out to the north of Whitby. In the thirteenth century, however, it was a fishing village – or rather two, East Row and Sandsend proper. Now it is a seaside paradise with soft sand, rockpools, wide open country and a gently sloping beach.

Lythe, just above Sandsend, also dates back to Saxon times. This is the Red Lion at the end of the 1980s.

Not much now remains of the Cistercian nunnery from which Rosedale Abbey got its name. At the heart of the North York Moors National Park, it owed its prosperity, both in the middle ages and in more recent times, to the presence of iron ore in the nearby hills. These two pictures from the late 1960s recall the time when Mace and Spar began the revolution in village shops, such as the Rosedale Abbey post office. Milk churns had been a feature of the countryside for generations before the advent of bulk tankers. The forest of TV aerials in the larger picture was caused by the need to have different ones for BBC and ITV.

Long before it was one of England's most elegant seaside resorts, Scarborough was a working fishing village. This photograph taken before the First World War and entitled 'Work and Gossip' shows the size of the fleet and just how important the industry was 100 years ago.

Tourism is by no means a new phenomenon in the town. Wordsworth and the Brontës were frequent visitors in the nineteenth century. Here people throng the footpaths and benches of the Italian Gardens in the 1920s.

The picture of the
donkeys on the sands is
even older than the
previous one, but the
between-the-wars
period was a golden
age for the English
seaside. Hoteliers,
caterers and
shopkeepers would rub
their hands to see this
number of people
promenading along the
North Sands or
relaxing at the Spa
seventy years on.

A spa town since the middle of the seventeenth century, Scarborough's origins go back much further. The Romans had a signal station here and the Normans built the castle in 1158. Scarborough claims to have invented the bathing machine in the eighteenth century – the town was certainly among the first to use one.

This is the way we know Scarborough today: neat pedestrianised streets lined with well-maintained buildings, and every possible feature and entertainment for visitors, whether families bound for the seaside, or politicos in conference.

The little market town of Selby is dwarfed by
the presence of the magnificent Selby 'Abbey'. It
is now really the parish church of Selby. By
becoming so at the time of the dissolution, it
managed to avoid the fate of Yorkshire's other
monastic buildings. Its central tower collapsed
in 1690 and it was damaged by fire in 1906, but
was fully rebuilt and restored.

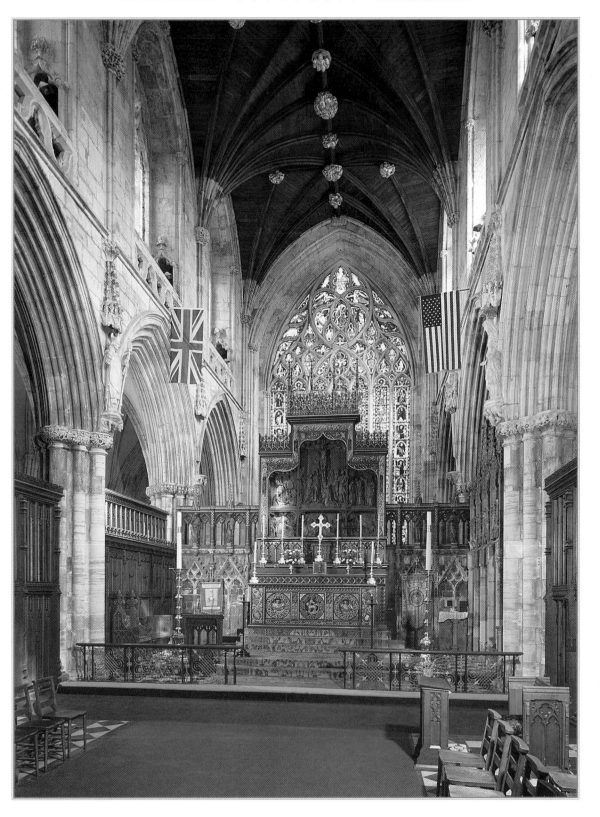

Below: This is a typical image of Sheffield at the height of its industrial power in the early years of the twentieth century. Affluence, from steel and from silver plate, had built grand Georgian houses and squares, but during the week the place was a hell-hole of smog, steam, fumes and noise.

On Sundays it all went quiet. For one day a week birdsong could be heard, the churchbells rang out and people could take a deep breath ready for it to all start again. Most of these chimneys are now gone and the centre of the city has been extensively altered, but the cathedral – on the right of the picture – has remained a landmark throughout all the changes, from the twelfth century to the present day.

Sheffield Cathedral was built as a parish church by one William de Lovetot, who seems to have been the first Norman lord of the town, despite the late date. Here it is in the 1970s, and it looks like rain.

A hundred years ago Sheffield was still in the heart of the countryside. This is a picturesque part of the Rivelin Valley. A Rivelin Valley Conservation Group was formed as recently as 1991.

Hathersage Bridge before the First World War.

The equally ancient bridge at Grindleford at the same time.

Grindleford Tunnel. This now forms part of the Hope Valley railway.

Jewel in Sheffield's crown, the Mappin Art Gallery was founded in 1887 in the grounds of
Weston Park to house the collection of the eponymous John Newton Mappin.
Sheffield's university was still a college of art when this photo was taken in the 1960s, as it
had been since 1843. In 1969 it admitted other disciplines and became one of Britain's first
polytechnics. Since 1992 it has been known as Sheffield Hallam University.

This is Sheffield City Hall in 1981. The 'City Clopper' horsebus is an old one used for publicity by Fletcher's Bread. Founded in 1923, Fletcher's was sold to Northern Foods in 1999.

Like Robin Hood's Bay, Staithes has paid a high price over the centuries for its exquisite position. Before the two stone breakwaters were built, destruction of its cottages by the sea was almost a routine event. Captain Cook spent his youth here before 'going for a sailor' in Whitby.

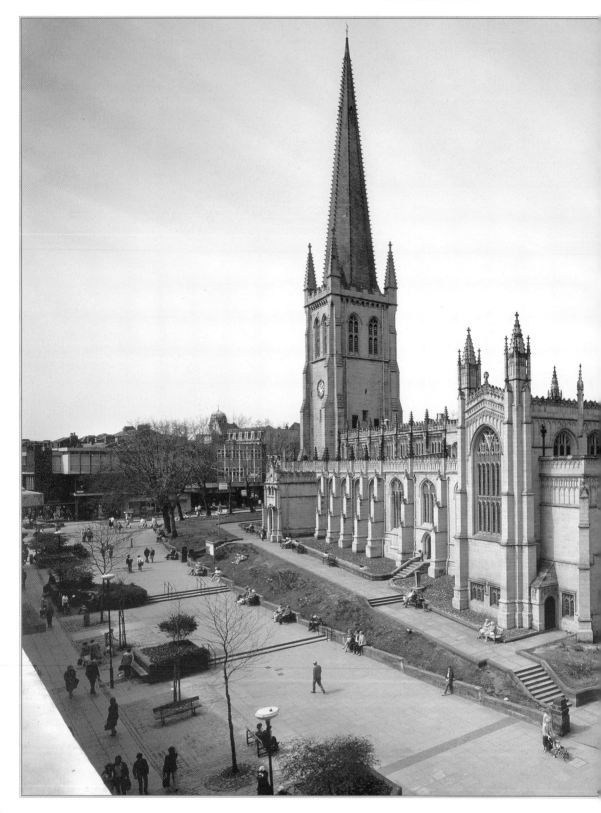

So neatly arranged it looks like a scene from a model village, this view of All Saints' church, Wakefield, dates from the late 1960s. At 247 feet, the graceful spire is the tallest in Yorkshire. The present city of Wakefield includes the old towns of Castleford and Pontefract.

Listed in Domesday as Torenten, Thornton-le-Dale had been established in a thorny dale by the Saxons. The Normans built their church here in the twelfth century and Sir Arthur Conan Doyle got married in it in 1885.

There's still plenty of water about in Thornton. For centuries it was a centre for milling of various kinds and activities that depended on it. There was a fulling mill, a paper mill and a flour mill run by the Burgess family, whose animal feeds business is pictured here in the 1960s, beyond the ford and the early D-series Citroën.

A market in Wetherby in the 1960s. Now the possessor of a fine bridge across the Wharfe, which forms part of the Great North Road, in Roman times it was also on the Military Way, which crossed the river at Helen's Ford. The town was in the possession of the mysterious Knights Templar for two hundred years before their order was outlawed by the pope in 1312.

A tranquil prospect of Whitby, half a century ago. St Mary's church is reached by climbing 199 steps. Its tower is Norman, but the nautical interior was created by local craftsmen in the eighteenth century.

Damaged not only by the usual ravages of time and plunder, Whitby Abbey was also shelled by the Germans. The original abbey on this site was founded in the seventh century, but the present ruins date from the thirteenth.

The Captain Cook Museum in Whitby contains this model of *Endeavour*, the ship in which the first Europeans discovered Australia. There is also a seagoing replica which, at this writing, is undergoing a refit in Cardiff.

A long time before these pictures were taken in the 1960s, Barnsley was Beorn's Lea, or meadow. For more than 500 years it was what lay beneath the lea that kept it going. It is at the heart of the South Yorkshire Coalfield.

There has been a market at Barnsley since 1249. Once you'd finished haggling, you could head across the road for a pint of Barnsley Bitter and a Capstan Full Strength.

Barnsley's College of Technology and its uncompromising building were joined by the local sixth form and art and design colleges to form Barnsley College in 1990.

Hull – or, more accurately, Kingston Upon Hull – is Britain's third largest seaport. The fishing port was established in the twelfth century by the Cistercians, but the town got its name when it passed to Edward I and he planned the new town there. These pictures convey the level of activity in this major seaway at the mouth of the Humber in the early years of the twentieth century. Its network of docks was built during the eighteenth and nineteenth centuries. This is the entrance to the Albert Dock.

This is another view of the Albert Dock, with some sizeable shipping and steam tugs lining the quay.

All movements were monitored from the Dock Offices, seen here from Prince's Dock. Cargo manifests would need to be delivered here for every item that entered or left the port. No computers in those days, but plenty of staff to check and double check the paperwork. Prince's Dock is now largely covered by the Prince's Quay shopping centre.

Here are two fishing smacks of the kind that made up the Hull fleet. The one in the foreground, *Jessie*, shows how much of the vessel was taken up with fish-carrying capacity.

This is the old Fish Quay. Many of the old dock areas have been built on in recent years.
The old Railway Dock and Humber Dock now form part of the marina.

The view to seaward from the Drypool Bridge on the River Hull. Nowadays there is the
Myton roadbridge to sweep motorists across the rivermouth. Southbridge Road is now
cut off, but retains its name as a memorial to the old crossing.

Rank's flour mills had been established here in the nineteenth century. They are still based near the old Drypool Bridge nowadays at the Clarence flour mills.

The mouth of the Hull River. The river was nearly as busy as the docks with the industries based there and further upriver.

Here's a typical riverside wharf with the old South Bridge beyond it.

Here's a view of the ruins in East Park. Hull suffered badly from Zeppelin raids in the
First World War and was the most badly damaged British town in the Second, with
92 per cent of its housing damaged by bombs.

Hull isn't all about those who go down to the sea in ships. It is a fine old city with some beautiful parks and gardens. This is West Park.

The Jowett car company was established in Bradford in 1910 – a year either way of this picture being taken. The company was the only British pioneer of the flat – 'boxer', or horizontally opposed – engine, used to good effect by Porsche, Volkswagen and Citroën.

Bradford's name came from 'broad ford'. Like many places in Yorkshire, it embraced the industrial revolution and went from a small rural town to an industrial powerhouse. In the mid-nineteenth century it was the wool capital of the world and went on to be an important engineering town, gaining city status in 1897. Its municipal waterworks, seen here, were built in the Ruritanian style.

Most people are now familiar with the bones of York's early history – Eboracum, the Roman city of the first century, became Jorvic, the Viking experience.

Because the people of this area gave the Normans so much trouble, William the Conqueror himself arrived in York and built two castles on the Ouse to keep them in order. One of these is what's now known as Clifford's Tower.

Fishergate Bar stands near the confluence of the Foss and the Ouse, in the south-eastern corner of the city, where it acted as a 'back gate', not being on any of the major routes.

A 'gate' in these parts is not a barrier, but a word from the same root as the Swedish 'gatan' or street. Hence Fossgate is the street that leads to the Foss river.

A 'bar' is a gate or barrier, as in the southern Potter's Bar (but not as in Ilkley Moor baht 'at, which is spelt differently). Walmgate Bar is a bar and a half, in that it retains its 'barbican' – a forward armoured gatehouse that protects the bar itself. The gatehouse was built in the twelfth century and the barbican added in the fourteenth.

The half-timbered extension to the Walmgate Bar was built in 1584. These 'spot-the-difference'-type pictures were taken from a similar angle, not that far apart, but one shows a balustrade on the roof and the other doesn't. From the fourteenth century this building was leased as a dwelling. The last tenants moved out in 1957!

Monk Bar was designed to be a self-contained fortress. The most elaborate of the remaining gates, it was built in the fourteenth century.

Built outside the city walls in the nineteenth century near Monk Bar on the bank above the moat, this brick igloo was an ice house. Ice was collected in winter and packed into it to provide refrigeration for food stored there.

Goodramgate was Guthrum's gate – named after a Viking lord.

When this first picture of Micklegate Bar was taken in the 1930s, there was one arch for road traffic and two for pedestrians.

Opposite: Long before this second picture, in the 1980s, the pavement was gone and the cars had it both ways. Micklegate Bar was the most important of York's gateways. A monarch visiting York has to stop here and ask permission of the Lord Mayor to enter the city.

Now an elegant shopping and residential street, Micklegate leads to the cathedral by
way of the Ousegate, Parliament Street and The Shambles.

Opposite: The very model of a medieval Minster. Petergate's jumbled buildings with
their attention focused on the heavenly finials is the ideal of the Christian middle ages.
Those arriving from Hull and Bridlington, Harrogate, Doncaster and somewhere called
London would get their first close-up of the Minster from here.

This picture from sixty years later gives a clearer image of the figures atop the gate, but cuts out the square where once was the horse trough, in order to omit the coach that occupies most of it.

Opposite: Bootham Bar and the Minster in the 1920s. Bootham Bar stands at one of the original Roman entrances to the city. The original gateway was built 2,000 years ago. The present gatehouse, like others, dates from the fourteenth century.

Stonegate was the direct
promenade to the Minster
for dignitaries from
the Guildhall and the
Lord Mayor from the
Mansion House. In the
old Roman days of
Eboracum, this was the
Via Praetoria – 'the way of
the magistrates, or
proconsuls'.

The Shambles was once the butchers' street in York. It has been claimed to be the best preserved medieval street in Europe, though this is somewhat doubtful. Certainly, if it still looked like this picture from the early part of the twentieth century, the claim would be strong.

It is still very beautiful, however, and on a scale that appeals to the human spirit. Its essence is perfectly captured in this night shot by John Edwards.

Although it has been saved from double yellow lines, satellite dishes and TV aerials, the profusion of written signs and the squaring up of the buildings has missed the point somewhere.

The building of the present York Minster embraced the three hundred years of perfection of gothic architecture from Early English to Perpendicular. Three previous cathedrals occupied the site, which helps to explain why it retains the Anglo-Saxon term Minster.

The Five Sisters window photographed in
around 1930 . . .

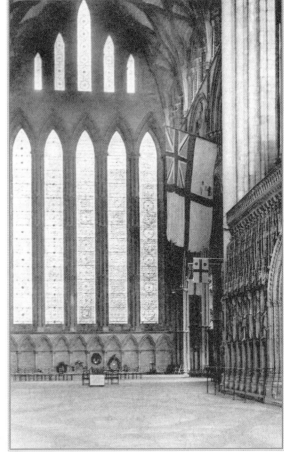

. . . and a ceiling boss benefiting from a modern
telephoto lens. York Minster is the largest gothic
church in England and contains the oldest
stained glass, some of it dating back over 800
years. In 1967 structural damage was discovered
beneath the central tower. Added in the fifteenth
century, this structure weighs around 20,000
tons and was in serious danger of collapse. The
engineering works involved in stabilising it
uncovered glories of its Roman and Saxon past,
which form part of the museum now housed in
the undercroft.